I0013170

POINTERS AND ARRAYS

Abhishek Dayal

Preface

If you want to be proficient in the writing of code in the C programming language, you must have a thorough working knowledge of how to use pointers. Unfortunately, C pointers appear to represent a stumbling block to newcomers, particularly those coming from other computer languages such as Fortran, Pascal or Basic.

To aid those newcomers in the understanding of pointers I have written the following material. To get the maximum benefit from this material, I feel it is important that the user be able to run the code in the various listings contained in the article. I have attempted, therefore, to keep all code ANSI compliant so that it will work with any ANSI compliant compiler. I have also tried to carefully block the code within the text. That way, with the help of an ASCII text editor, you can copy a given block of code to a new file and compile it on your system.

I recommend that readers do this as it will help in understanding the material.

ABHISHEK DAYAL

Maharashtra Institute of Technology, India

TABLE OF CONTENTS

PREFACE

CHAPTER 1:   What is a pointer?   1

CHAPTER 2:   Pointer types and Arrays   5

CHAPTER 3:   Pointers and Strings   12

CHAPTER 4:   More on Strings   15

CHAPTER 5:   Pointers and Structures   18

CHAPTER 6:   Some more on Strings, and Arrays of Strings   22

CHAPTER 7:   More on Multi-Dimensional Arrays   26

CHAPTER 8:   Pointers to Arrays   29

CHAPTER 9:   Pointers and Dynamic Allocation of Memory   31

CHAPTER 10:   Pointers to Functions   40

CHAPTER 1: What is a pointer?

One of those things beginners in C find difficult is the concept of pointers. The purpose of this tutorial is to provide an introduction to pointers and their use to these beginners. I have found that often the main reason beginners have a problem with pointers is that they have a weak or minimal feeling for variables, (as they are used in C). Thus we start with a discussion of C variables in general. A variable in a program is something with a name, the value of which can vary. The way the compiler and linker handles this is that it assigns a specific block of memory within the computer to hold the value of that variable. The size of that block depends on the range over which the variable is allowed to vary. For example, on PC's the size of an integer variable is 2 bytes, and that of a long integer is 4 bytes. In C the size of a variable type such as an integer need not be the same on all types of machines.

When we declare a variable we inform the compiler of two things, the name of the variable and the type of the variable. For example, we declare a variable of type integer with the name **k** by writing:

```
int k;
```

On seeing the "int" part of this statement the compiler sets aside 2 bytes of memory (on a PC) to hold the value of the integer. It also sets up a symbol table. In that table it adds the symbol **k** and the relative address in memory where those 2 bytes were set aside.

Thus, later if we write:

```
k = 2;
```

We expect that, at run time when this statement is executed, the value 2 will be placed in that memory location reserved for the storage of the value of **k**. In C we refer to a variable such as the integer **k** as an "object". In a sense there are two "values" associated with the object **k**. One is the value of the integer stored there (2 in the above example) and the other the "value" of the memory location, i.e., the address of **k**. Some texts refer to these two values with the nomenclature *rvalue* (right value, pronounced "are value") and *lvalue* (left value, pronounced "el value") respectively. In some languages, the lvalue is the value permitted on the left side of the assignment operator '=' (i.e. the address where the result of evaluation of the right side ends up). The rvalue is that which is on the right side of the assignment statement, the **2** above. Rvalues cannot be used on the left side of the assignment statement. Thus: **2 = k**; is illegal.

Actually, the above definition of "lvalue" is somewhat modified for C. According to K&R II (page 197): [1]

"An **object** is a named region of storage; an **lvalue** is an expression referring to an object."

However, at this point, the definition originally cited above is sufficient. As we become more familiar with pointers we will go into more detail on this.

Okay, now consider:

```
int j, k;
k = 2;
j = 7;   <-- line 1
k = j;   <-- line 2
```

In the above, the compiler interprets the **j** in line 1 as the address of the variable **j** (its lvalue) and creates code to copy the value 7 to that address. In line 2, however, the **j** is interpreted as its rvalue (since it is on the right hand side of the assignment operator '='). That is, here the **j** refers to the value **stored** at the memory location set aside for **j**, in this case 7. So, the 7 is copied to the address designated by the lvalue of **k**. In all of these examples, we are using 2 byte integers so all copying of rvalues from one storage location to the other is done by copying 2 bytes. Had we been using long integers, we would be copying 4 bytes. Now, let's say that we have a reason for wanting a variable designed to hold an lvalue (an address). The size required to hold such a value depends on the system. On older desk top computers with 64K of memory total, the address of any point in memory can be contained in 2 bytes. Computers with more memory would require more bytes to hold an address. Some computers, such as the IBM PC might require special handling to hold a segment and offset under certain circumstances. The actual size required is not too important so long as we have a way of informing the compiler that what we want to store is an address. Such a variable is called a **pointer variable** (for reasons which hopefully will become clearer a little later). In C when we define a pointer variable we do so by preceding its name with an asterisk. In C we also give our pointer a type which, in this case, refers to the type of data stored at the address we will be storing in our pointer. For example, consider the variable declaration:

```
int *ptr;
```

ptr is the name of our variable (just as **k** was the name of our integer variable). The '*' informs the compiler that we want a pointer variable, i.e. to set aside however many bytes is required to store an address in memory. The **int** says that we intend to use our pointer variable to store the address of an integer. Such a pointer is said to "point to" an integer.

However, note that when we wrote **int k;** we did not give **k** a value. If this definition is made outside of any function ANSI compliant compilers will initialize it to zero.

Similarly, **ptr** has no value, that is we haven't stored an address in it in the above declaration. In this case, again if the declaration is outside of any function, it is initialized to a value guaranteed in such a way that it is guaranteed to not point to any C object or function. A pointer initialized in this manner is called a "null" pointer.

The actual bit pattern used for a null pointer may or may not evaluate to zero since it depends on the specific system on which the code is developed. To make the source code compatible between various compilers on various systems, a macro is used to represent a null pointer. That macro goes under the name NULL. Thus, setting the value of a pointer using the NULL macro, as with an assignment statement such as ptr = NULL, guarantees that the pointer has become a null pointer. Similarly, just as one can test for an integer value of zero, as in **if(k == 0)**, we can test for a null pointer using **if (ptr == NULL)**.

But, back to using our new variable **ptr**. Suppose now that we want to store in **ptr** theaddress of our integer variable **k**. To do this we use the unary **&** operator and write:

```
ptr = &k;
```

What the **&** operator does is retrieve the lvalue (address) of **k**, even though **k** is on the right hand side of the assignment operator '=', and copies that to the contents of our pointer ptr. Now, ptr is said to "point to" **k**. Bear with us now, there is only one more operator we need to discuss.

The "dereferencing operator" is the asterisk and it is used as follows:

```
*ptr = 7;
```

will copy 7 to the address pointed to by **ptr**. Thus if **ptr** "points to" (contains the address of) **k**, the above statement will set the value of **k** to 7. That is, when we use the '*' this way we are referring to the value of that which ptr is pointing to, not the value of the pointer itself.

Similarly, we could write:

```
Printf("%d\n",*ptr);
```

to print to the screen the integer value stored at the address pointed to by **ptr**;. One way to see how all this stuff fits together would be to run the following program and then review the code and the output carefully.

```
------------ Program 1.1 ----------------------------
-----
/* Program 1.1 from PTRTUT10.TXT 6/10/97 */
#include <stdio.h>
int j, k;
int *ptr;
int main(void)
{
j = 1;
k = 2;
ptr = &k;
printf("\n");
printf("j has the value %d and is stored at %p\n", j,
(void *)&j);
printf("k has the value %d and is stored at %p\n", k,
(void *)&k);
printf("ptr has the value %p and is stored at %p\n",
ptr, (void *)&ptr);
printf("The value of the integer pointed to by ptr is
%d\n", *ptr);
return 0;
}
```

Note: We have yet to discuss those aspects of C which require the use of the
(void *) expression used here. For now, include it in your test code. We'll
explain the reason behind this expression later.

To review:

• A variable is declared by giving it a type and a name (e.g. **int k;**)

• A pointer variable is declared by giving it a type and a name (e.g. **int *ptr**)
where the asterisk tells the compiler that the variable named **ptr** is a pointer
variable and the type tells the compiler what type the pointer is to point to
(integer in this case).

• Once a variable is declared, we can get its address by preceding its name with
the unary **&** operator, as in **&k**.

• We can "dereference" a pointer, i.e. refer to the value of that which it points
to, by using the unary '*' operator as in ***ptr**.

• An "lvalue" of a variable is the value of its address, i.e. where it is stored in
memory. The "rvalue" of a variable is the value stored in that variable (at that
address).

CHAPTER 2: Pointer types and Arrays

Okay, let's move on. Let us consider why we need to identify the *type* of variable that a pointer points to, as in:

```
int *ptr;
```

One reason for doing this is so that later, once ptr "points to" something, if we write:

```
*ptr = 2;
```

the compiler will know how many bytes to copy into that memory location pointed to by **ptr**. If **ptr** was declared as pointing to an integer, 2 bytes would be copied, if a long, 4 bytes would be copied. Similarly for floats and doubles the appropriate number will be copied. But, defining the type that the pointer points to permits a number of other interesting ways a compiler can interpret code. For example, consider a block in memory consisting if ten integers in a row. That is, 20 bytes of memory are set aside to hold 10 integers.

Now, let's say we point our integer pointer **ptr** at the first of these integers. Furthermore let's say that integer is located at memory location 100 (decimal). What happens when we write:

```
ptr + 1;
```

Because the compiler "knows" this is a pointer (i.e. its value is an address) and that it points to an integer (its current address, 100, is the address of an integer), it adds 2 to **ptr** instead of 1, so the pointer "points to" the **next integer**, at memory location 102.

Similarly, were the **ptr** declared as a pointer to a long, it would add 4 to it instead of 1. The same goes for other data types such as floats, doubles, or even user defined data types such as structures. This is obviously not the same kind of "addition" that we normally think of. In C it is referred to as addition using "pointer arithmetic", a term which we will come back to later.

Similarly, since **++ptr** and **ptr++** are both equivalent to **ptr + 1** (though the point in the program when **ptr** is incremented may be different), incrementing a pointer using the unary ++ operator, either pre- or post-, increments the address it stores by the amount sizeof(type) where "type" is the type of the object pointed to. (i.e. 2 for an integer, 4 for a long, etc.).

Since a block of 10 integers located contiguously in memory is, by definition, an array of integers, this brings up an interesting relationship between arrays and pointers.

Consider the following:

```
int my_array[] = {1,23,17,4,-5,100};
```

Here we have an array containing 6 integers. We refer to each of these integers by means of a subscript to **my_array**, i.e. using **my_array[0]** through **my_array[5]**. But, we could alternatively access them via a pointer as follows:

```
int *ptr;
ptr = &my_array[0]; /* point our pointer at the first
integer in our array */
```

And then we could print out our array either using the array notation or by dereferencing our pointer. The following code illustrates this:

```
----------- Program 2.1 ------------------------------
------
/* Program 2.1 from PTRTUT10.HTM 6/13/97 */
#include <stdio.h>
int my_array[] = {1,23,17,4,-5,100};
int *ptr;
int main(void)
{
int i;
ptr = &my_array[0]; /* point our pointer to the first
element of the array */
printf("\n\n");
for (i = 0; i < 6; i++)
{
printf("my_array[%d] = %d ",i,my_array[i]); /*<-- A
*/
printf("ptr + %d = %d\n",i, *(ptr + i)); /*<-- B */
}
return 0;
}
```

Compile and run the above program and carefully note lines A and B and that the program prints out the same values in either case. Also observe how we dereferenced our pointer in line B, i.e. we first added i to it and then dereferenced the new pointer. Change line B to read:

```
printf("ptr + %d = %d\n",i, *ptr++);
```

and run it again... then change it to:

```
printf("ptr + %d = %d\n",i, *(++ptr));
```

and try once more. Each time try and predict the outcome and carefully look at the actual outcome.

In C, the standard states that wherever we might use **&var_name[0]** we can replace that with **var_name**, thus in our code where we wrote:

```
ptr = &my_array[0];
```

we can write:

```
ptr = my_array;
```

to achieve the same result.

This leads many texts to state that the name of an array is a pointer. I prefer to mentally think "the name of the array is the address of first element in the array". Many beginners (including myself when I was learning) have a tendency to become confused by thinking of it as a pointer. For example, while we can write

```
ptr = my_array;
```

we cannot write

```
my_array = ptr;
```

The reason is that while **ptr** is a variable, **my_array** is a constant. That is, the location at which the first element of **my_array** will be stored cannot be changed once **my_array[]** has been declared.Earlier when discussing the term "lvalue" I cited K&R-2 where it stated:"An **object** is a named region of storage; an **lvalue** is an expression referring to an object". This raises an interesting problem. Since **my_array** is a named region of storage, why is **my_array** in the above assignment statement not an lvalue? To resolve this problem, some refer to **my_array** as an "unmodifiable lvalue". Modify the example program above by changing

```
ptr = &my_array[0];
```

to

```
ptr = my_array;
```

and run it again to verify the results are identical.

Now, let's delve a little further into the difference between the names **ptr** and **my_array**as used above. Some writers will refer to an array's name as a *constant* pointer. What do we mean by that? Well, to understand the term "constant" in this sense, let's go back to our definition of the term "variable". When we declare a variable we set aside a spot in memory to hold the value of the appropriate type. Once that is done the name of the variable can be interpreted in one of two ways. When used on the left side of the assignment operator, the compiler interprets it as the memory location to which to move that value resulting from evaluation of the right side of the assignment operator. But, when used on the right side of the assignment operator, the name of a variable is interpreted to mean the contents stored at that memory address set aside to hold the value of that variable.

With that in mind, let's now consider the simplest of constants, as in:

```
int i, k;
i = 2;
```

Here, while **i** is a variable and then occupies space in the data portion of memory, **2** is a constant and, as such, instead of setting aside memory in the data segment, it is imbedded directly in the code segment of memory. That is, while writing something like **k = i;** tells the compiler to create code which at run time will look at memory location **&i** to determine the value to be moved to **k**, code created by **i = 2;** simply puts the **2** in the code and there is no referencing of the data segment. That is, both **k** and **i** are objects, but **2** is not an object.

Similarly, in the above, since **my_array** is a constant, once the compiler establishes where the array itself is to be stored, it "knows" the address of **my_array[0]** and on seeing:

```
ptr = my_array;
```

it simply uses this address as a constant in the code segment and there is no referencing of the data segment beyond that. This might be a good place explain further the use of the **(void *)** expression used in Program 1.1 of Chapter 1. As we have seen we can have pointers of various types. So far we have discussed pointers to integers and pointers to characters. In coming chapters we will be learning about pointers to structures and even pointer to pointers. Also we have learned that on different systems the size of a pointer can vary. As it turns out it is also possible that the size of a pointer can vary depending on the data type of the object to which it points. Thus, as with integers where you can run into trouble attempting to assign a long integer to a variable of type short integer, you can run into trouble attempting to assign the values of pointers of various types to pointer variables of other types.

To minimize this problem, C provides for a pointer of type void. We can declare such a pointer by writing:

```
void *vptr;
```

A void pointer is sort of a generic pointer. For example, while C will not permit the comparison of a pointer to type integer with a pointer to type character, for example, either of these can be compared to a void pointer. Of course, as with other variables, casts can be used to convert from one type of pointer to another under the proper circumstances. In Program 1.1. of Chapter 1 I cast the pointers to integers into void pointers to make them compatible with the %p conversion specification. In later chapters other casts will be made for reasons defined therein.

Well, that's a lot of technical stuff to digest and I don't expect a beginner to understand all of it on first reading. With time and experimentation you will want to come back and reread the first 2 chapters. But for now, let's move on to the relationship between pointers, character arrays, and strings.

CHAPTER 3: Pointers and Strings

The study of strings is useful to further tie in the relationship between pointers and arrays. It also makes it easy to illustrate how some of the standard C string functions can be implemented. Finally it illustrates how and when pointers can and should be passed to functions.

In C, strings are arrays of characters. This is not necessarily true in other languages. In BASIC, Pascal, Fortran and various other languages, a string has its own data type. But in C it does not. In C a string is an array of characters terminated with a binary zero character (written as '\0'). To start off our discussion we will write some code which, while preferred for illustrative purposes, you would probably never write in an actual program. Consider, for example:

```
char my_string[40];
my_string[0] = 'T';
my_string[1] = 'e';
my_string[2] = 'd':
my_string[3] = '\0';
```

While one would never build a string like this, the end result is a string in that it is an array of characters **terminated with a nul character**. By definition, in C, a string is an array of characters terminated with the nul character. Be aware that "nul" is **not** the same as "NULL". The nul refers to a zero as defined by the escape sequence '\0'. That is it occupies one byte of memory. NULL, on the other hand, is the name of the macro used to initialize null pointers. NULL is #defined in a header file in your C compiler, nul may not be #defined at all. Since writing the above code would be very time consuming, C permits two alternate ways of achieving the same thing. First, one might write:

```
char my_string[40] = {'T', 'e', 'd', '\0',};
```

But this also takes more typing than is convenient. So, C permits:

```
char my_string[40] = "Ted";
```

When the double quotes are used, instead of the single quotes as was done in the previous examples, the nul character ('\0') is automatically appended to the end of the string. In all of the above cases, the same thing happens. The compiler sets aside an contiguous block of memory 40 bytes long to hold characters and initialized it such that the first 4 characters are **Ted\0**.

Now, consider the following program:

```
--------------------program 3.1--------------------------
-------------
/* Program 3.1 from PTRTUT10.HTM 6/13/97 */
#include <stdio.h>
char strA[80] = "A string to be used for
demonstration purposes";
char strB[80];
int main(void)
{
char *pA; /* a pointer to type character */
char *pB; /* another pointer to type character */
puts(strA); /* show string A */
pA = strA; /* point pA at string A */
puts(pA); /* show what pA is pointing to */
pB = strB; /* point pB at string B */
putchar('\n'); /* move down one line on the screen */
while(*pA != '\0') /* line A (see text) */
{
*pB++ = *pA++; /* line B (see text) */
}
*pB = '\0'; /* line C (see text) */
puts(strB); /* show strB on screen */
return 0;
}
--------- end program 3.1 ---------------------------------
----------
```

In the above we start out by defining two character arrays of 80 characters each. Since these are globally defined, they are initialized to all '\0's first. Then, **strA** has the first 42 characters initialized to the string in quotes.

Now, moving into the code, we declare two character pointers and show the string on the screen. We then "point" the pointer **pA** at **strA**. That is, by means of the assignment statement we copy the address of **strA[0]** into our variable **pA**. We now use **puts()** to show that which is pointed to by **pA** on the screen. Consider here that the function prototype for **puts()** is:

```
int puts(const char *s);
```

For the moment, ignore the **const**. The parameter passed to **puts()** is a pointer, that is the **value** of a pointer (since all parameters in C are passed by value), and the value of a pointer is the address to which it points, or, simply, an address. Thus when we write **puts(strA);** as we have seen, we are passing the address of **strA[0]**.

Similarly, when we write **puts(pA);** we are passing the same address, since we have set **pA = strA;**

Given that, follow the code down to the **while()** statement on line A. Line A states: While the character pointed to by **pA** (i.e. ***pA**) is not a nul character (i.e. the terminating '\0'), do the following: Line B states: copy the character pointed to by **pA** to the space pointed to by **pB**, then increment **pA** so it points to the next character and **pB** so it points to the next space.

When we have copied the last character, **pA** now points to the terminating nul character and the loop ends. However, we have not copied the nul character. And, by definition a string in C **must** be nul terminated. So, we add the nul character with line C.

It is very educational to run this program with your debugger while watching **strA**, **strB**, **pA** and **pB** and single stepping through the program. It is even more educational if instead of simply defining **strB[]** as has been done above, initialize it also with something like:

```
strB[80] =
"12345678901234567890123456789012345678901234567890"
```

where the number of digits used is greater than the length of **strA** and then repeat the single stepping procedure while watching the above variables. Give these things a try!

Getting back to the prototype for **puts()** for a moment, the "const" used as a parameter modifier informs the user that the function will not modify the string pointed to by **s**, i.e. it will treat that string as a constant.

Of course, what the above program illustrates is a simple way of copying a string. After playing with the above until you have a good understanding of what is happening, we can proceed to creating our own replacement for the standard **strcpy()** that comes with C. It might look like:

```
char *my_strcpy(char *destination, char *source)
{
char *p = destination;
while (*source != '\0')
{
*p++ = *source++;
}
*p = '\0';
return destination;
```

```
}
```

In this case, I have followed the practice used in the standard routine of returning a pointer to the destination.
Again, the function is designed to accept the values of two character pointers, i.e. addresses, and thus in the previous program we could write:

```
int main(void)
{
my_strcpy(strB, strA);
puts(strB);
}
```

I have deviated slightly from the form used in standard C which would have the prototype:

```
char *my_strcpy(char *destination, const char
*source);
```

Here the "const" modifier is used to assure the user that the function will not modify the contents pointed to by the source pointer. You can prove this by modifying the function above, and its prototype, to include the "const" modifier as shown. Then, within the function you can add a statement which attempts to change the contents of that which is pointed to by source, such as:

```
*source = 'X';
```

which would normally change the first character of the string to an X. The const modifier should cause your compiler to catch this as an error. Try it and see. Now, let's consider some of the things the above examples have shown us. First off, consider the fact that ***ptr++** is to be interpreted as returning the value pointed to by **ptr** and then incrementing the pointer value. This has to do with the precedence of the operators. Were we to write **(*ptr)++** we would increment, not the pointer, but that which the pointer points to! i.e. if used on the first character of the above example string the 'T' would be incremented to a 'U'. You can write some simple example code to illustrate this. Recall again that a string is nothing more than an array of characters, with the last character being a '\0'. What we have done above is deal with copying an array. It happens to be an array of characters but the technique could be applied to an array of integers, doubles, etc. In those cases, however, we would not be dealing with strings and hence the end of the array would not be marked with a special value like the nul character. We could implement a version that relied on a special value to identify the end. For example, we could copy an array of positive integers by marking the end with a negative integer.

On the other hand, it is more usual that when we write a function to copy an array of items other than strings we pass the function the number of items to be copied as well as the address of the array, e.g. something like the following prototype might indicate:

```
void int_copy(int *ptrA, int *ptrB, int nbr);
```

where **nbr** is the number of integers to be copied. You might want to play with this idea and create an array of integers and see if you can write the function **int_copy()** and make it work.

This permits using functions to manipulate large arrays. For example, if we have an array of 5000 integers that we want to manipulate with a function, we need only pass to that function the address of the array (and any auxiliary information such as nbr above, depending on what we are doing). The array itself does **not** get passed, i.e. the whole array is not copied and put on the stack before calling the function, only its address is sent.

This is different from passing, say an integer, to a function. When we pass an integer we make a copy of the integer, i.e. get its value and put it on the stack. Within the function any manipulation of the value passed can in no way effect the original integer. But, with arrays and pointers we can pass the address of the variable and hence manipulate the values of the original variables.

CHAPTER 4: More on Strings

Well, we have progressed quite a way in a short time! Let's back up a little and look at what was done in Chapter 3 on copying of strings but in a different light. Consider the following function:

```
char *my_strcpy(char dest[], char source[])
{
int i = 0;
while (source[i] != '\0')
{
dest[i] = source[i];
i++;
}
dest[i] = '\0';
return dest;
}
```

Recall that strings are arrays of characters. Here we have chosen to use array notation instead of pointer notation to do the actual copying. The results are the same, i.e. the string gets copied using this notation just as accurately as it did before. This raises some interesting points which we will discuss.

Since parameters are passed by value, in both the passing of a character pointer or the name of the array as above, what actually gets passed is the address of the first element of each array. Thus, the numerical value of the parameter passed is the same whether we use a character pointer or an array name as a parameter. This would tend to imply that somehow **source[i]** is the same as ***(p+i)**.

In fact, this is true, i.e wherever one writes **a[i]** it can be replaced with ***(a + i)** without any problems. In fact, the compiler will create the same code in either case. Thus we see that pointer arithmetic is the same thing as array indexing. Either syntax produces the same result.

This is NOT saying that pointers and arrays are the same thing, they are not. We are only saying that to identify a given element of an array we have the choice of two syntaxes, one using array indexing and the other using pointer arithmetic, which yield identical results.

Now, looking at this last expression, part of it.. **(a + i)**, is a simple addition using the + operator and the rules of C state that such an expression is commutative. That is **(a + i)** is identical to **(i + a)**. Thus we could write ***(i + a)** just as easily as ***(a + i)**.

But ***(i + a)** could have come from **i[a]** ! From all of this comes the curious truth that if:

```
char a[20];
int i;
```

writing

```
a[3] = 'x';
```

is the same as writing

```
3[a] = 'x';
```

Try it! Set up an array of characters, integers or longs, etc. and assigned the 3rd or 4th element a value using the conventional approach and then print out that value to be sure you have that working. Then reverse the array notation as I have done above. A good compiler will not balk and the results will be identical. A curiosity... nothing more!

Now, looking at our function above, when we write:

```
dest[i] = source[i];
```

due to the fact that array indexing and pointer arithmetic yield identical results, we can write this as:

```
*(dest + i) = *(source + i);
```

But, this takes 2 additions for each value taken on by i. Additions, generally speaking, take more time than incrementations (such as those done using the **++** operator as in **i++**). This may not be true in modern optimizing compilers, but one can never be sure. Thus, the pointer version may be a bit faster than the array version. Another way to speed up the pointer version would be to change:

```
while (*source != '\0')
```

to simply

```
while (*source)
```

since the value within the parenthesis will go to zero (FALSE) at the same time in either case.

At this point you might want to experiment a bit with writing some of your own programs using pointers. Manipulating strings is a good place to experiment. You might want to write your own versions of such standard functions as:

```
strlen();
```

```
strcat();
strchr();
```

and any others you might have on your system. We will come back to strings
and their manipulation through pointers in a future chapter. For now, let's move
on and discuss structures for a bit.

CHAPTER 5: Pointers and Structures

As you may know, we can declare the form of a block of data containing different data types by means of a structure declaration. For example, a personnel file might contain structures which look something like:

```
struct tag
{
char lname[20]; /* last name */
char fname[20]; /* first name */
int age; /* age */
float rate; /* e.g. 12.75 per hour */
};
```

Let's say we have a bunch of these structures in a disk file and we want to read each one out and print out the first and last name of each one so that we can have a list of the people in our files. The remaining information will not be printed out. We will want to do this printing with a function call and pass to that function a pointer to the structure at hand. For demonstration purposes I will use only one structure for now. But realize the goal is the writing of the function, not the reading of the file which, presumably, we know how to do.

For review, recall that we can access structure members with the dot operator as in:

```
--------------- program 5.1 ------------------
/* Program 5.1 from PTRTUT10.HTM 6/13/97 */
#include <stdio.h>
#include <string.h>
struct tag {
char lname[20]; /* last name */
char fname[20]; /* first name */
int age; /* age */
float rate; /* e.g. 12.75 per hour */
};
struct tag my_struct; /* declare the structure
my_struct */
int main(void)
{
strcpy(my_struct.lname,"Jensen");
strcpy(my_struct.fname,"Ted");
```

```
printf("\n%s ",my_struct.fname);
printf("%s\n",my_struct.lname);
return 0;
}
-------------- end of program 5.1 --------------
```

Now, this particular structure is rather small compared to many used in C programs. To the above we might want to add:

```
date_of_hire;  (data types not shown)
date_of_last_raise;
last_percent_increase;
emergency_phone;
medical_plan;
Social_S_Nbr;
etc.....
```

If we have a large number of employees, what we want to do is manipulate the data in these structures by means of functions. For example we might want a function print out the name of the employee listed in any structure passed to it. However, in the original C (Kernighan & Ritchie, 1st Edition) it was not possible to pass a structure, only a pointer to a structure could be passed. In ANSI C, it is now permissible to pass the complete structure. But, since our goal here is to learn more about pointers, we won't pursue that.
Anyway, if we pass the whole structure it means that we must copy the contents of the structure from the calling function to the called function. In systems using stacks, this is done by pushing the contents of the structure on the stack. With large structures this could prove to be a problem. However, passing a pointer uses a minimum amount of stack space.
In any case, since this is a discussion of pointers, we will discuss how we go about passing a pointer to a structure and then using it within the function. Consider the case described, i.e. we want a function that will accept as a parameter a pointer to a structure and from within that function we want to access members of the structure. For example we want to print out the name of the employee in our example structure.
Okay, so we know that our pointer is going to point to a structure declared using struct tag. We declare such a pointer with the declaration:

```
struct tag *st_ptr;
```

and we point it to our example structure with:

```
st_ptr = &my_struct;
```

Now, we can access a given member by de-referencing the pointer. But, how do we dereference the pointer to a structure? Well, consider the fact that we might want to use the pointer to set the age of the employee. We would write:

```
(*st_ptr).age = 63;
```

Look at this carefully. It says, replace that within the parenthesis with that which **st_ptr** points to, which is the structure **my_struct**. Thus, this breaks down to the same as **my_struct.age**.
However, this is a fairly often used expression and the designers of C have created an alternate syntax with the same meaning which is:

```
st_ptr->age = 63;
```

With that in mind, look at the following program:

```
------------- program 5.2 ----------------------
/* Program 5.2 from PTRTUT10.HTM 6/13/97 */
#include <stdio.h>
#include <string.h>
struct tag{ /* the structure type */
char lname[20]; /* last name */
char fname[20]; /* first name */
int age; /* age */
float rate; /* e.g. 12.75 per hour */
};
struct tag my_struct; /* define the structure */
void show_name(struct tag *p); /* function prototype
*/
int main(void)
{
struct tag *st_ptr; /* a pointer to a structure */
st_ptr = &my_struct; /* point the pointer to
my_struct */
strcpy(my_struct.lname,"Jensen");
strcpy(my_struct.fname,"Ted");
printf("\n%s ",my_struct.fname);
printf("%s\n",my_struct.lname);
my_struct.age = 63;
show_name(st_ptr); /* pass the pointer */
return 0;
}
```

```
void show_name(struct tag *p)
{
printf("\n%s ", p->fname); /* p points to a structure
*/
printf("%s ", p->lname);
printf("%d\n", p->age);
}
----------------- end of program 5.2 -------------
```

Again, this is a lot of information to absorb at one time. The reader should compile and run the various code snippets and using a debugger monitor things like **my_struct** and **p** while single stepping through the main and following the code down into the function to see what is happening.

CHAPTER 6: Some more on Strings, and Arrays of Strings

Well, let's go back to strings for a bit. In the following all assignments are to be understood as being global, i.e. made outside of any function, including main(). We pointed out in an earlier chapter that we could write:

```
char my_string[40] = "Ted";
```

which would allocate space for a 40 byte array and put the string in the first 4 bytes (three for the characters in the quotes and a 4th to handle the terminating '\0'). Actually, if all we wanted to do was store the name "Ted" we could write:

```
char my_name[] = "Ted";
```

and the compiler would count the characters, leave room for the nul character and store the total of the four characters in memory the location of which would be returned by the array name, in this case **my_name**.
In some code, instead of the above, you might see:

```
char *my_name = "Ted";
```

which is an alternate approach. Is there a difference between these? The answer is.. yes. Using the array notation 4 bytes of storage in the static memory block are taken up, one for each character and one for the terminating nul character. But, in the pointer notation the same 4 bytes required, **plus** N bytes to store the pointer variable **my_name** (where N depends on the system but is usually a minimum of 2 bytes and can be 4 or more). In the array notation, **my_name** is short for **&myname[0]** which is the address of the first element of the array. Since the location of the array is fixed during run time, this is a constant (not a variable). In the pointer notation **my_name** is a variable. As to which is the **better** method, that depends on what you are going to do within the rest of the program. Let's now go one step further and consider what happens if each of these declarations are done within a function as opposed to globally outside the bounds of any function.

```
void my_function_A(char *ptr)
{
char a[] = "ABCDE"
```

```
.
}
void my_function_B(char *ptr)
{
char *cp = "FGHIJ"
.
.
.
}
```

In the case of **my_function_A**, the content, or value(s), of the array **a[]** is considered to be the data. The array is said to be initialized to the values ABCDE. In the case of **my_function_B**, the value of the pointer **cp** is considered to be the data. The pointer has been initialized to point to the string **FGHIJ**. In both **my_function_A** and **my_function_B** the definitions are local variables and thus the string **ABCDE** is stored on the stack, as is the value of the pointer **cp**. The string **FGHIJ** can be stored anywhere. On my system it gets stored in the data segment. By the way, array initialization of automatic variables as I have done in **my_function_A** was illegal in the older K&R C and only "came of age" in the newer ANSI C. A fact that may be important when one is considering portability and backwards compatibility. As long as we are discussing the relationship/differences between pointers and arrays, let's move on to multi-dimensional arrays. Consider, for example the array:

```
char multi[5][10];
```

Just what does this mean? Well, let's consider it in the following light.

```
char multi[5][10];
```

Let's take the underlined part to be the "name" of an array. Then prepending the **char** and appending the **[10]** we have an array of 10 characters. But, the name **multi[5]** is itself an array indicating that there are 5 elements each being an array of 10 characters. Hence we have an array of 5 arrays of 10 characters each..

Assume we have filled this two dimensional array with data of some kind. In memory, it might look as if it had been formed by initializing 5 separate arrays using something like:

```
multi[0] = {'0','1','2','3','4','5','6','7','8','9'}
multi[1] = {'a','b','c','d','e','f','g','h','i','j'}
multi[2] = {'A','B','C','D','E','F','G','H','I','J'}
multi[3] = {'9','8','7','6','5','4','3','2','1','0'}
multi[4] = {'J','I','H','G','F','E','D','C','B','A'}
```

At the same time, individual elements might be addressable using syntax such as:

```
multi[0][3] = '3'
multi[1][7] = 'h'
multi[4][0] = 'J'
```

Since arrays are contiguous in memory, our actual memory block for the above should look like:

```
0123456789abcdefghijABCDEFGHIJ9876543210JIHGFEDCBA
^
|_____   starting at the address &multi[0][0]
```

Note that I did **not** write **multi[0] = "0123456789"**. Had I done so a terminating **'\0'** would have been implied since whenever double quotes are used a **'\0'** character is appended to the characters contained within those quotes. Had that been the case I would have had to set aside room for 11 characters per row instead of 10. My goal in the above is to illustrate how memory is laid out for 2 dimensional arrays. That is, this is a 2 dimensional array of characters, NOT an array of "strings".

Now, the compiler knows how many columns are present in the array so it can interpret **multi + 1** as the address of the 'a' in the 2nd row above. That is, it adds 10, the number of columns, to get this location. If we were dealing with integers and an array with the same dimension the compiler would add **10*sizeof(int)** which, on my machine, would be 20.

Thus, the address of the **9** in the 4th row above would be **&multi[3][0]** or ***(multi + 3)** in

pointer notation. To get to the content of the 2nd element in the 4th row we add 1 to this address and dereference the result as in

```
*(*(multi + 3) + 1)
```

With a little thought we can see that:

```
*(*(multi + row) + col) and
multi[row][col] yield the same results.
```

The following program illustrates this using integer arrays instead of character arrays.

```
------------------ program 6.1 ---------------------
-
/* Program 6.1 from PTRTUT10.HTM 6/13/97*/
#include <stdio.h>
#define ROWS 5
#define COLS 10
int multi[ROWS][COLS];
int main(void)
{
int row, col;
for (row = 0; row < ROWS; row++)
{
for (col = 0; col < COLS; col++)
{
multi[row][col] = row*col;
}
```

29

```
}
for (row = 0; row < ROWS; row++)
{
for (col = 0; col < COLS; col++)
{
printf("\n%d ",multi[row][col]);
printf("%d ",*(*(multi + row) + col));
}
}
return 0;
}
--------------- end of program 6.1 ----------------
```

Because of the double de-referencing required in the pointer version, the name of a 2 dimensional array is often said to be equivalent to a pointer to a pointer. With a three dimensional array we would be dealing with an array of arrays of arrays and some might say its name would be equivalent to a pointer to a pointer to a pointer. However, here we have initially set aside the block of memory for the array by defining it using array notation. Hence, we are dealing with a constant, not a variable. That is we are talking about a fixed address not a variable pointer. The dereferencing function used above permits us to access any element in the array of arrays without the need of changing the value of that address (the address of **multi[0][0]** as given by the symbol **multi**).

CHAPTER 7: More on Multi-Dimensional Arrays

In the previous chapter we noted that given

```
#define ROWS 5
#define COLS 10
int multi[ROWS][COLS];
```

we can access individual elements of the array **multi** using either:

```
multi[row][col]
```

or

```
*(*(multi + row) + col)
```

To understand more fully what is going on, let us replace

```
*(multi + row)
```

with **X** as in:

```
*(X + col)
```

Now, from this we see that **X** is like a pointer since the expression is de-referenced and we know that **col** is an integer. Here the arithmetic being used is of a special kind called "pointer arithmetic" is being used. That means that, since we are talking about an integer array, the address pointed to by (i.e. value of) **X + col + 1** must be greater than the address **X + col** by and amount equal to **sizeof(int)**.

Since we know the memory layout for 2 dimensional arrays, we can determine that in the expression **multi + row** as used above, **multi + row + 1** must increase by value an amount equal to that needed to "point to" the next row, which in this case would be an amount equal to **COLS * sizeof(int)**.

That says that if the expression ***(*(multi + row) + col)** is to be evaluated correctly at run time, the compiler must generate code which takes into consideration the value of **COLS**, i.e. the 2nd dimension. Because of the equivalence of the two forms of expression, this is true whether we are using the pointer expression as here or the array expression **multi[row][col]**.

Thus, to evaluate either expression, a total of 5 values must be known:

1. The address of the first element of the array, which is returned by the expression **multi**, i.e., the name of the array.
2. The size of the type of the elements of the array, in this case **sizeof(int)**.
3. The 2nd dimension of the array
4. The specific index value for the first dimension, **row** in this case.
5. The specific index value for the second dimension, **col** in this case.

Given all of that, consider the problem of designing a function to manipulate the element values of a previously declared array. For example, one which would set all the elements of the array **multi** to the value 1.

```
void set_value(int m_array[][COLS])
{
int row, col;
for (row = 0; row < ROWS; row++)
{
for (col = 0; col < COLS; col++)
{
m_array[row][col] = 1;
}
}
}
```

And to call this function we would then use:

```
set_value(multi);
```

Now, within the function we have used the values #defined by ROWS and COLS that set the limits on the for loops. But, these #defines are just constants as far as the compiler is concerned, i.e. there is nothing to connect them to the array size within the function. **Row** and **col** are local variables, of course. The formal parameter definition permits the compiler to determine the characteristics associated with the pointer value that will be passed at run time. We really don't need the first dimension and, as will be seen later, there are occasions where we would prefer not to define it within the parameter definition, out of habit or consistency, I have not used it here. But, the second dimension must be used as has been shown in the expression for the parameter. The reason is that we need this in the evaluation of **m_array[row][col]** as has been described. While the parameter defines the data type (**int** in this case) and the automatic variables for row and column are defined in the for loops, only one value can be passed using a single parameter. In this case, that is the value of **multi** as noted in the call statement, i.e. the address of the first element, often referred to as a pointer to the array. Thus, the only way we have of informing the compiler of the 2nd dimension is by explicitly including it in the parameter definition.

In fact, in general all dimensions of higher order than one are needed when dealing with multi-dimensional arrays. That is if we are talking about 3 dimensional arrays, the 2nd **and** 3rd dimension must be specified in the parameter definition.

CHAPTER 8: Pointers to Arrays

Pointers, of course, can be "pointed at" any type of data object, including arrays. While that was evident when we discussed program 3.1, it is important to expand on how we do this when it comes to multi-dimensional arrays.
To review, in Chapter 2 we stated that given an array of integers we could point an integer pointer at that array using:

```
int *ptr;
ptr = &my_array[0]; /* point our pointer at the first
integer in our array */
```

As we stated there, the type of the pointer variable must match the type of the first element of the array.
In addition, we can use a pointer as a formal parameter of a function which is designed to manipulate an array. e.g. Given:

```
int array[3] = {'1', '5', '7'};
void a_func(int *p);
```

Some programmers might prefer to write the function prototype as:

```
void a_func(int p[]);
```

which would tend to inform others who might use this function that the function is designed to manipulate the elements of an array. Of course, in either case, what actually gets passed is the value of a pointer to the first element of the array, independent of which notation is used in the function prototype or definition. Note that if the array notation is used, there is no need to pass the actual dimension of the array since we are not passing the whole array, only the address to the first element. We now turn to the problem of the 2 dimensional array. As stated in the last chapter, C interprets a 2 dimensional array as an array of one dimensional arrays. That being the case, the first element of a 2 dimensional array of integers is a one dimensional array of integers. And a pointer to a two dimensional array of integers must be a pointer to that data type. One way of accomplishing this is through the use of the keyword "typedef". typedef assigns a new name to a specified data type. For example:

```
typedef unsigned char byte;
```

causes the name **byte** to mean type **unsigned char**. Hence

```
byte b[10]; would be an array of unsigned characters.
```

Note that in the typedef declaration, the word **byte** has replaced that which would normally be the name of our **unsigned char**. That is, the rule for using **typedef** is that the new name for the data type is the name used in the definition of the data type. Thus in:

```
typedef int Array[10];
```

Array becomes a data type for an array of 10 integers. i.e. **Array my_arr;** declares **my_arr** as an array of 10 integers and **Array arr2d[5];** makes **arr2d** an array of 5 arrays of 10 integers each. Also note that **Array *p1d;** makes **p1d** a pointer to an array of 10 integers. Because ***p1d** points to the same type as **arr2d**, assigning the address of the two dimensional array **arr2d** to **p1d**, the pointer to a one dimensional array of 10 integers is acceptable. i.e. **p1d = &arr2d[0];** or **p1d = arr2d;** are both correct.

Since the data type we use for our pointer is an array of 10 integers we would expect that incrementing **p1d** by 1 would change its value by **10*sizeof(int)**, which it does. That is, **sizeof(*p1d)** is 20. You can prove this to yourself by writing and running a simple short program.

Now, while using typedef makes things clearer for the reader and easier on the programmer, it is not really necessary. What we need is a way of declaring a pointer like **p1d** without the need of the **typedef** keyword. It turns out that this can be done and that

```
int (*p1d)[10];
```

is the proper declaration, i.e. **p1d** here is a pointer to an array of 10 integers just as it was under the declaration using the Array type. Note that this is different from

```
int *p1d[10];
```

which would make **p1d** the name of an array of 10 pointers to type **int**.

CHAPTER 9: Pointers and Dynamic Allocation of Memory

There are times when it is convenient to allocate memory at run time using **malloc()**, **calloc()**, or other allocation functions. Using this approach permits postponing the decision on the size of the memory block need to store an array, for example, until run time. Or it permits using a section of memory for the storage of an array of integers at one point in time, and then when that memory is no longer needed it can be freed up for other uses, such as the storage of an array of structures. When memory is allocated, the allocating function (such as **malloc()**, **calloc()**, etc) returns a pointer. The type of this pointer depends on whether you are using an older K&R compiler or the newer ANSI type compiler. With the older compiler the type of the returned pointer is **char**, with the ANSI compiler it is **void**. If you are using an older compiler, and you want to allocate memory for an array of integers you will have to cast the char pointer returned to an integer pointer. For example, to allocate space for 10 integers we might write:

```
int *iptr;
iptr = (int *)malloc(10 * sizeof(int));
if (iptr == NULL)
{ .. ERROR ROUTINE GOES HERE .. }
```

If you are using an ANSI compliant compiler, **malloc()** returns a **void** pointer and since a void pointer can be assigned to a pointer variable of any object type, the **(int *)** cast shown above is not needed. The array dimension can be determined at run time and is not needed at compile time. That is, the **10** above could be a variable read in from a data file or keyboard, or calculated based on some need, at run time. Because of the equivalence between array and pointer notation, once **iptr** has been assigned as above, one can use the array notation. For example, one could write:

```
int k;
for (k = 0; k < 10; k++)
iptr[k] = 2;
```

to set the values of all elements to 2.

Even with a reasonably good understanding of pointers and arrays, one place the newcomer to C is likely to stumble at first is in the dynamic allocation of multidimensional arrays. In general, we would like to be able to access elements of such arrays using array notation, not pointer notation, wherever possible. Depending on the application we may or may not know both dimensions at compile time. This leads to a variety of ways to go about our task.

As we have seen, when dynamically allocating a one dimensional array its dimension can be determined at run time. Now, when using dynamic allocation of higher order arrays, we never need to know the first dimension at compile time. Whether we need to know the higher dimensions depends on how we go about writing the code. Here I will discuss various methods of dynamically allocating room for 2 dimensional arrays of integers. First we will consider cases where the 2nd dimension is known at compile time.

METHOD 1:

One way of dealing with the problem is through the use of the **typedef** keyword. To allocate a 2 dimensional array of integers recall that the following two notations result in the same object code being generated:

```
multi[row][col] = 1;  *(*(multi + row) + col) = 1;
```

It is also true that the following two notations generate the same code:

```
multi[row]  *(multi + row)
```

Since the one on the right must evaluate to a pointer, the array notation on the left must also evaluate to a pointer. In fact **multi[0]** will return a pointer to the first integer in the first row, **multi[1]** a pointer to the first integer of the second row, etc. Actually, **multi[n]** evaluates to a pointer to that array of integers that make up the n-th row of our 2 dimensional array. That is, **multi** can be thought of as an array of arrays and **multi[n]** as a pointer to the n-th array of this array of arrays. Here the word **pointer** is being used to represent an address value. While such usage is common in the literature, when reading such statements one must be careful to distinguish between the constant address of an array and a variable pointer which is a data object in itself.
Consider now:

```
---------------- Program 9.1 --------------------
/* Program 9.1 from PTRTUT10.HTM 6/13/97 */
#include <stdio.h>
#include <stdlib.h>
#define COLS 5
typedef int RowArray[COLS];
RowArray *rptr;
int main(void)
```

```
{
int nrows = 10;
int row, col;
rptr = malloc(nrows * COLS * sizeof(int));
for (row = 0; row < nrows; row++)
36
{
for (col = 0; col < COLS; col++)
{
rptr[row][col] = 17;
}
}
return 0;
}
-------------- End of Prog. 9.1 -----------------
```

Here I have assumed an ANSI compiler so a cast on the void pointer returned by **malloc()** is not required. If you are using an older K&R compiler you will have to cast using:

```
rptr = (RowArray *)malloc(.... etc.
```

Using this approach, **rptr** has all the characteristics of an array name name, (except that rptr is modifiable), and array notation may be used throughout the rest of the program. That also means that if you intend to write a function to modify the array contents, you must use COLS as a part of the formal parameter in that function, just as we did when discussing the passing of two dimensional arrays to a function.

METHOD 2:

In the METHOD 1 above, rptr turned out to be a pointer to type "one dimensional array of COLS integers". It turns out that there is syntax which can be used for this type without the need of **typedef**. If we write:

```
int (*xptr)[COLS];
```

the variable **xptr** will have all the same characteristics as the variable **rptr** in METHOD 1 above, and we need not use the **typedef** keyword. Here **xptr** is a pointer to an array of integers and the size of that array is given by the **#defined COLS**. The parenthesis placement makes the pointer notation predominate, even though the array notation has higher precedence. i.e. had we written

```
int *xptr[COLS];
```

We would have defined **xptr** as an array of pointers holding the number of pointers equal to that #defined by COLS. That is not the same thing at all. However, arrays of pointers have their use in the dynamic allocation of two dimensional arrays, as will be seen in the next 2 methods.

METHOD 3:

Consider the case where we do not know the number of elements in each row at compile time, i.e. both the number of rows and number of columns must be determined at run time. One way of doing this would be to create an array of pointers to type **int** and then allocate space for each row and point these pointers at each row. Consider:

```
--------------- Program 9.2 -----------------
/* Program 9.2 from PTRTUT10.HTM 6/13/97 */
#include <stdio.h>
#include <stdlib.h>
int main(void)
{
int nrows = 5; /* Both nrows and ncols could be
evaluated */
int ncols = 10; /* or read in at run time */
int row;
int **rowptr;
rowptr = malloc(nrows * sizeof(int *));
if (rowptr == NULL)
{
puts("\nFailure to allocate room for row
pointers.\n");
exit(0);
}
printf("\n\n\nIndex Pointer(hex) Pointer(dec)
Diff.(dec)");
for (row = 0; row < nrows; row++)
{
rowptr[row] = malloc(ncols * sizeof(int));
if (rowptr[row] == NULL)
{
printf("\nFailure to allocate for row[%d]\n",row);
exit(0);
}
printf("\n%d %p %d", row, rowptr[row],
rowptr[row]);
```

```
            if (row > 0)
            printf(" %d",(int)(rowptr[row] - rowptr[row-1]));
            }
        return 0;
        }
```
--------------- End 9.2 --------------------

In the above code **rowptr** is a pointer to pointer to type **int**. In this case it points to the first element of an array of pointers to type **int**. Consider the number of calls to **malloc()**:

```
To get the array of pointers 1 call
To get space for the rows 5 calls
-----
Total 6 calls
```

If you choose to use this approach note that while you can use the array notation to access individual elements of the array, e.g. **rowptr[row][col] = 17;**, it does not mean that the data in the "two dimensional array" is contiguous in memory.

You can, however, use the array notation just as if it were a continuous block of memory.
For example, you can write:

```
rowptr[row][col] = 176;
```

just as if rowptr were the name of a two dimensional array created at compile time. Of course **row** and **col** must be within the bounds of the array you have created, just as with an array created at compile time.
If you want to have a contiguous block of memory dedicated to the storage of the elements in the array you can do it as follows:

METHOD 4:
In this method we allocate a block of memory to hold the whole array first. We then create an array of pointers to point to each row. Thus even though the array of pointers is being used, the actual array in memory is contiguous. The code looks like this:

```
------------------ Program 9.3 ------------------
/* Program 9.3 from PTRTUT10.HTM 6/13/97 */
#include <stdio.h>
#include <stdlib.h>
int main(void)
{
```

```c
int **rptr;
int *aptr;
int *testptr;
int k;
int nrows = 5; /* Both nrows and ncols could be
evaluated */
int ncols = 8; /* or read in at run time */
int row, col;
/* we now allocate the memory for the array */
aptr = malloc(nrows * ncols * sizeof(int));
if (aptr == NULL)
{
puts("\nFailure to allocate room for the array");
exit(0);
}
/* next we allocate room for the pointers to the rows
*/
rptr = malloc(nrows * sizeof(int *));
if (rptr == NULL)
{
puts("\nFailure to allocate room for pointers");
exit(0);
}
```

39

```c
/* and now we 'point' the pointers */
for (k = 0; k < nrows; k++)
{
rptr[k] = aptr + (k * ncols);
}
/* Now we illustrate how the row pointers are
incremented */
printf("\n\nIllustrating how row pointers are
incremented");
printf("\n\nIndex Pointer(hex) Diff.(dec)");
for (row = 0; row < nrows; row++)
{
printf("\n%d %p", row, rptr[row]);
if (row > 0)
printf(" %d",(rptr[row] - rptr[row-1]));
}
printf("\n\nAnd now we print out the array\n");
for (row = 0; row < nrows; row++)
{
```

```
for (col = 0; col < ncols; col++)
{
rptr[row][col] = row + col;
printf("%d ", rptr[row][col]);
}
putchar('\n');
}
puts("\n");
/* and here we illustrate that we are, in fact,
dealing with
a 2 dimensional array in a contiguous block of
memory. */
printf("And now we demonstrate that they are
contiguous in
memory\n");
testptr = aptr;
for (row = 0; row < nrows; row++)
{
for (col = 0; col < ncols; col++)
{
printf("%d ", *(testptr++));
}
putchar('\n');
}
return 0;
}
-------------- End Program 9.3 ------------------
```

Consider again, the number of calls to malloc()

```
To get room for the array itself 1 call
To get room for the array of ptrs 1 call
----
Total 2 calls
```

Now, each call to **malloc()** creates additional space overhead since **malloc()** is generally implemented by the operating system forming a linked list which contains data concerning the size of the block. But, more importantly, with large arrays (several hundred rows) keeping track of what needs to be freed when the time comes can be more cumbersome. This, combined with the contiguousness of the data block that permits initialization to all zeroes using **memset()** would seem to make the second alternative the preferred one.

As a final example on multidimensional arrays we will illustrate the dynamic allocation of a three dimensional array. This example will illustrate one more thing to watch when doing this kind of allocation. For reasons cited above we will use the approach outlined in alternative two. Consider the following code:

```
------------------- Program 9.4 ----------------
/* Program 9.4 from PTRTUT10.HTM 6/13/97 */
#include <stdio.h>
#include <stdlib.h>
#include <stddef.h>
int X_DIM=16;
int Y_DIM=5;
int Z_DIM=3;
int main(void)
{
char *space;
char ***Arr3D;
int y, z;
ptrdiff_t diff;
/* first we set aside space for the array itself */
space = malloc(X_DIM * Y_DIM * Z_DIM * sizeof(char));
/* next we allocate space of an array of pointers, each
to eventually point to the first element of a
2 dimensional array of pointers to pointers */
Arr3D = malloc(Z_DIM * sizeof(char **));
/* and for each of these we assign a pointer to a newly
allocated array of pointers to a row */
for (z = 0; z < Z_DIM; z++)
{
Arr3D[z] = malloc(Y_DIM * sizeof(char *));
/* and for each space in this array we put a pointer to
the first element of each row in the array space
originally allocated */
41
for (y = 0; y < Y_DIM; y++)
{
Arr3D[z][y] = space + (z*(X_DIM * Y_DIM) + y*X_DIM);
}
}
```

```
/* And, now we check each address in our 3D array to
see if
the indexing of the Arr3d pointer leads through in a
continuous manner */
for (z = 0; z < Z_DIM; z++)
{
printf("Location of array %d is %p\n", z, *Arr3D[z]);
for ( y = 0; y < Y_DIM; y++)
{
printf(" Array %d and Row %d starts at %p", z, y,
Arr3D[z][y]);
diff = Arr3D[z][y] - space;
printf(" diff = %d ",diff);
printf(" z = %d y = %d\n", z, y);
}
}
return 0;
}
------------------ End of Prog. 9.4 ----------------
```

If you have followed this tutorial up to this point you should have no problem deciphering the above on the basis of the comments alone. There are a couple of points that should be made however. Let's start with the line which reads:

```
Arr3D[z][y] = space + (z*(X_DIM * Y_DIM) + y*X_DIM);
```

Note that here **space** is a character pointer, which is the same type as **Arr3D[z][y]**. It is important that when adding an integer, such as that obtained by evaluation of the expression **(z*(X_DIM * Y_DIM) + y*X_DIM)**, to a pointer, the result is a new pointer value. And when assigning pointer values to pointer variables the data types of the value and variable must match.

CHAPTER 10: Pointers to Functions

Up to this point we have been discussing pointers to data objects. C also permits the mdeclaration of pointers to functions. Pointers to functions have a variety of uses and some of them will be discussed here.

Consider the following real problem. You want to write a function that is capable of sorting virtually any collection of data that can be stored in an array. This might be an array of strings, or integers, or floats, or even structures. The sorting algorithm can be the same for all. For example, it could be a simple bubble sort algorithm, or the more complex shell or quick sort algorithm. We'll use a simple bubble sort for demonstration purposes. Sedgewick [1] has described the bubble sort using C code by setting up a function which when passed a pointer to the array would sort it. If we call that function **bubble()**, a sort program is described by bubble_1.c, which follows

```
/*------------------- bubble_1.c -----------------*/
/* Program bubble_1.c from PTRTUT10.HTM 6/13/97 */
#include <stdio.h>
int arr[10] = { 3,6,1,2,3,8,4,1,7,2};
void bubble(int a[], int N);
int main(void)
{
int i;
putchar('\n');
for (i = 0; i < 10; i++)
{
printf("%d ", arr[i]);
}
bubble(arr,10);
putchar('\n');
for (i = 0; i < 10; i++)
{
printf("%d ", arr[i]);
}
return 0;
}
void bubble(int a[], int N)
{
int i, j, t;
for (i = N-1; i >= 0; i--)
```

```
{
for (j = 1; j <= i; j++)
43
{
if (a[j-1] > a[j])
{
t = a[j-1];
a[j-1] = a[j];
a[j] = t;
}
}
}
}
/*----------------- end bubble_1.c -----------------*/
```

The bubble sort is one of the simpler sorts. The algorithm scans the array from
the second to the last element comparing each element with the one which
precedes it. If the one that precedes it is larger than the current element, the two
are swapped so the larger one is closer to the end of the array. On the first pass,
this results in the largest element ending up at the end of the array. The array is
now limited to all elements except the last and the process repeated. This puts
the next largest element at a point preceding the largest element. The process is
repeated for a number of times equal to the number of elements minus 1. The
end result is a sorted array. Here our function is designed to sort an array of
integers. Thus in line 1 we are comparing integers and in lines 2 through 4 we
are using temporary integer storage to store integers. What we want to do now
is see if we can convert this code so we can use any data type, i.e. not be
restricted to integers.

At the same time we don't want to have to analyze our algorithm and the code
associated with it each time we use it. We start by removing the comparison
from within the function **bubble()** so as to make it relatively easy to modify the
comparison function without having to re-write portions related to the actual
algorithm. This results in bubble_2.c:

```
/*----------------- bubble_2.c -----------------*/
/* Program bubble_2.c from PTRTUT10.HTM 6/13/97 */
/* Separating the comparison function */
#include <stdio.h>
int arr[10] = { 3,6,1,2,3,8,4,1,7,2};
void bubble(int a[], int N);
int compare(int m, int n);
int main(void)
{
```

```c
int i;
putchar('\n');
for (i = 0; i < 10; i++)
{
printf("%d ", arr[i]);
}
bubble(arr,10);
putchar('\n');
for (i = 0; i < 10; i++)
{
printf("%d ", arr[i]);
}
return 0;
}
void bubble(int a[], int N)
{
int i, j, t;
for (i = N-1; i >= 0; i--)
{
for (j = 1; j <= i; j++)
{
if (compare(a[j-1], a[j]))
{
t = a[j-1];
a[j-1] = a[j];
a[j] = t;
}
}
}
}
int compare(int m, int n)
{
return (m > n);
}
/*--------------- end of bubble_2.c ---------------*/
```

If our goal is to make our sort routine data type independent, one way of doing this is to use pointers to type void to point to the data instead of using the integer data type. As a start in that direction let's modify a few things in the above so that pointers can be used. To begin with, we'll stick with pointers to type integer.

```c
/*------------------- bubble_3.c -------------------*/
```

```c
/* Program bubble_3.c from PTRTUT10.HTM 6/13/97 */
#include <stdio.h>
int arr[10] = { 3,6,1,2,3,8,4,1,7,2};
void bubble(int *p, int N);
int compare(int *m, int *n);
int main(void)
{
int i;
putchar('\n');
for (i = 0; i < 10; i++)
{
printf("%d ", arr[i]);
}
bubble(arr,10);
putchar('\n');
for (i = 0; i < 10; i++)
{
printf("%d ", arr[i]);
}
return 0;
}
void bubble(int *p, int N)
{
int i, j, t;
for (i = N-1; i >= 0; i--)
{
for (j = 1; j <= i; j++)
{
if (compare(&p[j-1], &p[j]))
{
t = p[j-1];
p[j-1] = p[j];
p[j] = t;
}
}
}
}
int compare(int *m, int *n)
{
return (*m > *n);
}
/*--------------- end of bubble3.c ---------------*/
```

Note the changes. We are now passing a pointer to an integer (or array of integers) to **bubble()**. And from within bubble we are passing pointers to the elements of the array that we want to compare to our comparison function. And, of course we are dereferencing these pointer in our **compare()** function in order to make the actual comparison. Our next
step will be to convert the pointers in **bubble()** to pointers to type void so that that function will become more type insensitive. This is shown in bubble_4.

```c
/*----------------- bubble_4.c ------------------*/
/* Program bubble_4.c from PTRTUT10,HTM 6/13/97 */
#include <stdio.h>
int arr[10] = { 3,6,1,2,3,8,4,1,7,2};
void bubble(int *p, int N);
int compare(void *m, void *n);
int main(void)
{
int i;
putchar('\n');
for (i = 0; i < 10; i++)
{
printf("%d ", arr[i]);
}
bubble(arr,10);
putchar('\n');
for (i = 0; i < 10; i++)
{
printf("%d ", arr[i]);
}
return 0;
}
void bubble(int *p, int N)
{
int i, j, t;
for (i = N-1; i >= 0; i--)
{
for (j = 1; j <= i; j++)
{
if (compare((void *)&p[j-1], (void *)&p[j]))
{
t = p[j-1];
p[j-1] = p[j];
p[j] = t;
}
```

```
        }
      }
    }
    int compare(void *m, void *n)
    {
    int *m1, *n1;
    m1 = (int *)m;
    n1 = (int *)n;
    return (*m1 > *n1);
    }
    /*----------- end of bubble_4.c ----------------*/
```

Note that, in doing this, in **compare()** we had to introduce the casting of the void pointer types passed to the actual type being sorted. But, as we'll see later that's okay. And since what is being passed to **bubble()** is still a pointer to an array of integers, we had to cast these pointers to void pointers when we passed them as parameters in our call to **compare()**.

We now address the problem of what we pass to **bubble()**. We want to make the first parameter of that function a void pointer also. But, that means that within **bubble()** we need to do something about the variable **t**, which is currently an integer. Also, where we use **t = p[j-1];** the type of **p[j-1]** needs to be known in order to know how many bytes to copy to the variable **t** (or whatever we replace **t** with). Currently, in bubble_4.c, knowledge within **bubble()** as to the type of the data being sorted (and hence the size of each individual element) is obtained from the fact that the first parameter is a pointer to type integer. If we are going to be able to use **bubble()** to sort any type of data, we need to make that pointer a pointer to type **void**. But, in doing so we are going to lose information concerning the size of individual elements within the array. So, in bubble_5.c we will add a separate parameter to handle this size information. These changes, from bubble4.c to bubble5.c are, perhaps, a bit more extensive than those we have made in the past. So, compare the two modules carefully for differences.

```
    /*----------------- bubble5.c ----------------------*/
    /* Program bubble_5.c from PTRTUT10.HTM 6/13/97 */
    #include <stdio.h>
    #include <string.h>
    long arr[10] = { 3,6,1,2,3,8,4,1,7,2};
    void bubble(void *p, size_t width, int N);
    int compare(void *m, void *n);
    int main(void)
    {
    int i;
    putchar('\n');
```

```c
    for (i = 0; i < 10; i++)
    {
    printf("%d ", arr[i]);
    }
    bubble(arr, sizeof(long), 10);
    putchar('\n');
    for (i = 0; i < 10; i++)
    {
    printf("%ld ", arr[i]);
    }
    return 0;
    }
    void bubble(void *p, size_t width, int N)
    {
    int i, j;
    unsigned char buf[4];
    unsigned char *bp = p;
48
    for (i = N-1; i >= 0; i--)
    {
    for (j = 1; j <= i; j++)
    {
    if (compare((void *)(bp + width*(j-1)),
    (void *)(bp + j*width))) /* 1 */
    {
    /* t = p[j-1]; */
    memcpy(buf, bp + width*(j-1), width);
    /* p[j-1] = p[j]; */
    memcpy(bp + width*(j-1), bp + j*width , width);
    /* p[j] = t; */
    memcpy(bp + j*width, buf, width);
    }
    }
    }
    }
    int compare(void *m, void *n)
    {
    long *m1, *n1;
    m1 = (long *)m;
    n1 = (long *)n;
    return (*m1 > *n1);
    }
/*---------------- end of bubble5.c --------------*/
```

Note that I have changed the data type of the array from **int** to **long** to illustrate the changes needed in the **compare()** function. Within **bubble()** I've done away with the variable **t** (which we would have had to change from type **int** to type **long**). I have added a buffer of size 4 unsigned characters, which is the size needed to hold a long (this will change again in future modifications to this code). The unsigned character pointer ***bp** is used to point to the base of the array to be sorted, i.e. to the first element of that array. We also had to modify what we passed to **compare()**, and how we do the swapping of elements that the comparison indicates need swapping. Use of **memcpy()** and pointer notation instead of array notation work towards this reduction in type sensitivity. Again, making a careful comparison of bubble5.c with bubble4.c can result in improved understanding of what is happening and why. We move now to bubble6.c where we use the same function bubble() that we used in bubble5.c to sort strings instead of long integers. Of course we have to change the comparison function since the means by which strings are compared is different from that by which long integers are compared. And, in bubble6.c we have deleted the lines within **bubble()** that were commented out in bubble5.c.

```c
/*------------------ bubble6.c --------------------*/
/* Program bubble_6.c from PTRTUT10.HTM 6/13/97 */
#include <stdio.h>
#include <string.h>
#define MAX_BUF 256
char arr2[5][20] = { "Mickey Mouse",
"Donald Duck",
"Minnie Mouse",
"Goofy",
"Ted Jensen" };
void bubble(void *p, int width, int N);
int compare(void *m, void *n);
int main(void)
{
int i;
putchar('\n');
for (i = 0; i < 5; i++)
{
printf("%s\n", arr2[i]);
}
bubble(arr2, 20, 5);
putchar('\n\n');
for (i = 0; i < 5; i++)
{
printf("%s\n", arr2[i]);
```

```c
}
return 0;
}
void bubble(void *p, int width, int N)
{
int i, j, k;
unsigned char buf[MAX_BUF];
unsigned char *bp = p;
for (i = N-1; i >= 0; i--)
{
for (j = 1; j <= i; j++)
{
k = compare((void *)(bp + width*(j-1)), (void *)(bp +
j*width));
if (k > 0)
{
memcpy(buf, bp + width*(j-1), width);
memcpy(bp + width*(j-1), bp + j*width , width);
memcpy(bp + j*width, buf, width);
}
}
}
}
int compare(void *m, void *n)
```

50

```c
{
char *m1 = m;
char *n1 = n;
return (strcmp(m1,n1));
}
/*--------------- end of bubble6.c ----------------*/
```

But, the fact that **bubble()** was unchanged from that used in bubble5.c indicates that that function is capable of sorting a wide variety of data types. What is left to do is to pass to **bubble()** the name of the comparison function we want to use so that it can be truly universal. Just as the name of an array is the address of the first element of the array in the data segment, the name of a function decays into the address of that function in the code segment. Thus we need to use a pointer to a function. In this case the comparison function. Pointers to functions must match the functions pointed to in the number and types of the parameters and the type of the return value. In our case, we declare our function pointer as:

```c
int (*fptr)(const void *p1, const void *p2);
```

Note that were we to write:

```
int *fptr(const void *p1, const void *p2);
```

we would have a function prototype for a function which returned a pointer to type **int**.

That is because in C the parenthesis () operator have a higher precedence than the pointer * operator. By putting the parenthesis around the string (*fptr) we indicate that we are declaring a function pointer. We now modify our declaration of **bubble()** by adding, as its 4th parameter, a function pointer of the proper type. It's function prototype becomes:

```
void bubble(void *p, int width, int N,
int(*fptr)(const void *, const void *));
```

When we call the **bubble()**, we insert the name of the comparison function that we want to use. bubble7.c illustrate how this approach permits the use of the same **bubble()** function for sorting different types of data.

```
/*------------------- bubble7.c -------------------*/
/* Program bubble_7.c from PTRTUT10.HTM 6/10/97 */
#include <stdio.h>
#include <string.h>
#define MAX_BUF 256
51
long arr[10] = { 3,6,1,2,3,8,4,1,7,2};
char arr2[5][20] = { "Mickey Mouse",
"Donald Duck",
"Minnie Mouse",
"Goofy",
"Ted Jensen" };
void bubble(void *p, int width, int N,
int(*fptr)(const void *, const void *));
int compare_string(const void *m, const void *n);
int compare_long(const void *m, const void *n);
int main(void)
{
int i;
puts("\nBefore Sorting:\n");
for (i = 0; i < 10; i++) /* show the long ints */
{
printf("%ld ",arr[i]);
```

```c
}
puts("\n");
for (i = 0; i < 5; i++) /* show the strings */
{
printf("%s\n", arr2[i]);
}
bubble(arr, 4, 10, compare_long); /* sort the longs
*/
bubble(arr2, 20, 5, compare_string); /* sort the
strings */
puts("\n\nAfter Sorting:\n");
for (i = 0; i < 10; i++) /* show the sorted longs */
{
printf("%d ",arr[i]);
}
puts("\n");
for (i = 0; i < 5; i++) /* show the sorted strings */
{
printf("%s\n", arr2[i]);
}
return 0;
}
void bubble(void *p, int width, int N,
int (*fptr)(const void *, const void *))
{
int i, j, k;
unsigned char buf[MAX_BUF];
unsigned char *bp = p;
for (i = N-1; i >= 0; i--)
{
for (j = 1; j <= i; j++)
{
k = fptr((void *)(bp + width*(j-1)), (void *)(bp +
j*width));
```
52
```c
if (k > 0)
{
memcpy(buf, bp + width*(j-1), width);
memcpy(bp + width*(j-1), bp + j*width , width);
memcpy(bp + j*width, buf, width);
}
}
}
```

```c
}
int compare_string(const void *m, const void *n)
{
char *m1 = (char *)m;
char *n1 = (char *)n;
return (strcmp(m1,n1));
}
int compare_long(const void *m, const void *n)
{
long *m1, *n1;
m1 = (long *)m;
n1 = (long *)n;
return (*m1 > *n1);
}
/*-------------- end of bubble7.c ----------------*/
```